Penguin Readers

AF099421

LIAR'S BEACH

KATIE COTUGNO

LEVEL

RETOLD BY SAFFRON DODD
ILLUSTRATED BY OLEG BUYEVSKY
SERIES EDITOR: SORREL PITTS

Contains adult content, which could include: sexual behaviour or exploitation, misuse of alcohol, smoking, illegal drugs, violence and dangerous behaviour.

PENGUIN BOOKS

UK | USA | Canada | Ireland | Australia
India | New Zealand | South Africa

Penguin Books is part of the Penguin Random House group of companies whose addresses can be found at global.penguinrandomhouse.com.
www.penguin.co.uk www.puffin.co.uk www.ladybird.co.uk

Liar's Beach first published by Penguin Books Ltd, 2023
This Penguin Readers edition published by Penguin Books Ltd, 2026
001

Original text written by Katie Cotugno
Text for Penguin Readers edition adapted by Saffron Dodd
Original copyright © Katie Cotugno and Alloy Entertainment, 2023
Text for Penguin Readers edition copyright © Penguin Books Ltd, 2026
Illustrated by Oleg Buyevsky
Illustrations copyright © Penguin Books Ltd, 2026
Cover image copyright © Ewelina Dymek, 2023

The moral right of the original author has been asserted

Penguin Random House values and supports copyright. Copyright fuels creativity, encourages diverse voices, promotes freedom of expression and supports a vibrant culture. Thank you for purchasing an authorized edition of this book and for respecting intellectual property laws by not reproducing, scanning or distributing any part of it by any means without permission. You are supporting authors and enabling Penguin Random House to continue to publish books for everyone. No part of this book may be used or reproduced in any manner for the purpose of training artificial intelligence technologies or systems. In accordance with Article 4(3) of the DSM Directive 2019/790, Penguin Random House expressly reserves this work from the text and data mining exception.

Printed and bound in Great Britain by Clays Ltd, Elcograf S.p.A.

The authorized representative in the EEA is Penguin Random House Ireland, Morrison Chambers, 32 Nassau Street, Dublin D02 YH68

A CIP catalogue record for this book is available from the British Library

ISBN: 978–0–241–75394–1

All correspondence to:
Penguin Books
Penguin Random House Children's
One Embassy Gardens, 8 Viaduct Gardens,
London SW11 7BW

 Penguin Random House is committed to a sustainable future for our business, our readers and our planet. This book is made from Forest Stewardship Council® certified paper.

Contents

People in the story	4
New words	5
Note about the story	6
Before-reading questions	6
Chapter One — The house	7
Chapter Two — Lies	14
Chapter Three — The fight	20
Chapter Four — Suspects	27
Chapter Five — The sweater	33
Chapter Six — Wells's secret	42
Chapter Seven — Topher	50
Chapter Eight — Hurricane party	58
Chapter Nine — The truth	66
During-reading questions	72
After-reading questions	73
Exercises	74
Project work	77
Glossary	78

People in the story

Michael Linden

Jasper and Eliza Kendrick

Meredith

Greg

Aidy

Holiday

New words

ambulance

island

jail

necklace

pool

waitress

Note about the story

Liar's Beach is Katie Cotugno's first murder **mystery*** book. The story is about a boy called Linden and his visit to his friend's beach house on an island called Martha's Vineyard. Many people in Martha's Vineyard are very rich, but Linden's family is not. Linden has rich friends because he has a sports **scholarship** to an expensive school. *Liar's Beach* is a story about friends, money, secrets, love, and **lies**.

Before-reading questions

1 Read the title of this book and look at the cover. What will this book be about, do you think?

2 Martha's Vineyard is an island in the United States of America with many big beach houses. What people live on Martha's Vineyard, do you think? Are they rich or poor? What schools do their children go to? What are their lives like?

3 This is a story about secrets. Do you have secrets? Do you tell your secrets to anyone?

4 Look at the "People in the story" on page 4 and choose two characters. What are they like, do you think?

*Definitions of words in **bold** can be found in the glossary on pages 78–80.

CHAPTER ONE
The house

Ten days before the police came to August House and we were on the news, Jasper met me at the boat.

"I thought that you were coming last night." he said. He wore sunglasses and a white shirt.

I climbed into his expensive car. "The boat was full," I said. This was a **lie**. The **truth** was that I had to work at my supermarket job. I often **lied** to Jasper and our rich friends at our expensive **boarding** school about money.

I lied to them about other things, too.

"How was your summer job?" Jasper asked.

"What? Oh. It was fine," I said.

Jasper thought that I had an important **law** job. It was a stupid lie, but I did not want Jasper to know that my family was **working class**. We did not have much money to pay for my boarding school. But I was smart, and I was good at a sport called lacrosse, so I had a **scholarship**.

Jasper drove us down a long road. We were on an island called Martha's Vineyard, and at the end of the road was a beach and a beautiful large white house.

"This is August House," Jasper said.

"Wow!" I thought, but I didn't say it. I didn't want Jasper to know that his house and money **impressed** me.

I took my bag and I followed Jasper into the garden. There was a large pool with two boys in it and some steps that went down to the beach.

"Linden is here," Jasper said.

"Hey," said the first boy. He was Jasper's older brother, Wells. Wells pointed to the other boy in the pool. "That's Doc. He lives in a house down the beach."

"And do you know my sister, Eliza?" Jasper pointed at a girl.

I did know Eliza. Eliza lived at home with her parents, but we met once or twice when she came to our boarding school to see Jasper. She was sitting on a chair by the pool next to another girl with red hair. Eliza waved at me. She was wearing sunglasses and a bikini.

I waved back.

I liked Eliza.

"And I'm Meredith," said the girl with red hair.

Jasper looked at Meredith. "Yes. That's Meredith. Now, I want to show you the house." I followed Jasper into the house. We walked into a hall and saw a sleeping dog.

"That's Whimsy," said Jasper. He touched Whimsy gently and smiled. "Follow me, Linden. I'll show you your room."

We walked through the huge dining room into the living room, and then a library. Then, we passed a study and went up lots of stairs.

"Meredith lived near here once," Jasper told me. "But her parents sold their house last year. They don't have a house on the beach any more, so she comes here every day."

Jasper didn't sound happy about this.

"Did you two ever **date**?" I asked.

"No," said Jasper quickly. "She has a boyfriend called Greg. I don't like Meredith or Greg."

Jasper's parents took us into town for a fish dinner that night. When we walked to the cars, Mrs. Kendrick put her hand on my arm.

"Linden," she said. "Thank you for being a good friend to Jasper."

"He's a good friend to me too," I said.

"Yes," said Mrs. Kendrick. "But this was a difficult year for Jasper. It was hard for all of us."

"OK," I said, but I thought, "What is she talking about? Did something bad happen?"

I knew that Jasper's dad had some trouble with the law last year, but I didn't like to ask my friends questions about their lives. This was because I didn't want them to ask questions about mine.

We were eating at a restaurant called Red's. While we waited for a table, Eliza turned to me.

"Are you from Boston?" she asked.

"Yes. I was born there," I said, but I did not say any more. I did not want her to know I lived in the poorer part of Boston in a small and old apartment.

"Do you like football?" she asked.

"Not really," I answered. "I like lacrosse more."

"Oh yes," said Mr. Kendrick. "How is your leg, Linden? Are you going to play lacrosse in the fall?"

"Dad, don't," said Jasper. "Linden doesn't want to talk about that."

"It's OK," I said. I hurt my leg in a car **crash** six months ago with a girl I was dating. Her name was Greer.

"My leg is fine now," I said.

That was another lie because my leg still hurt. But I needed to play lacrosse to keep my scholarship.

"You're a good player," said Mr. Kendrick.

I just smiled.

Our waitress came with our food. She was blonde and pretty. Jasper smiled at her, but Meredith didn't.

"Can I have another cola?" Meredith asked.

"Of course," said the waitress. She walked away.

"Oh, sorry," said Meredith, when the waitress came back. "Can I have some lemon in it?" But Meredith didn't sound sorry.

"OK," said the waitress. She smiled at Meredith but it was not a nice smile. "Is that everything?"

"Yes it is—for now," said Meredith.

The waitress walked away. Jasper looked angry. "Why are you being so **rude**?"

"I'm not being rude," said Meredith. Then, she

waved her hand at the waitress and shouted, "I want another knife!"

That night, we had a small party on the beach with some of Jasper's friends.

"There you are!" Doc said when he saw us. "I'm happy that you came."

"Of course," said Eliza. She smiled at Doc, and I suddenly felt a bit **jealous**.

I spoke to some of Jasper's friends from Martha's Vineyard, and then I sat down on the beach.

"You're quiet," said Eliza. She sat next to me and gave me a bottle of beer. "Are you OK?"

"I just like to watch people sometimes," I said.

"Are you watching me, Linden?"

"Why?" I asked with a **grin**. "Do you want me to watch you?"

"Maybe," Eliza said. She **grinned** back at me.

Eliza was a beautiful girl. I was planning to say, "Do you want to go for a walk with me?" but then someone said my name loudly.

"Michael?"

I turned around quickly. Only my mom and one other person called me by my first name.

CHAPTER TWO
Lies

"Holiday," I said. "Hello."

My mom worked for Holiday's parents. She cleaned their huge house in Boston and cooked their meals.

"Hi!" said Holiday happily. She looked different. She still had her dark curly hair and glasses, but she looked older and prettier.

I last saw Holiday three years ago — before I started boarding school.

"What are you doing here?" she asked me.

"I'm staying with friends from school," I said. I pointed at Eliza, Jasper, and Meredith.

Holiday waved at them, but I quickly pulled her away down the beach. "What are you doing here?" I asked.

"My parents have a beach house here on the island," she said. "Didn't your mom tell you?"

"No," I said. This was another lie. She told me, but I didn't think it was important enough to remember. I needed to get away from Holiday. I didn't want Eliza or Jasper to know that my mother worked for Holiday's parents.

"Well, it was nice to see you. I have to go back to my friends now," I told her.

At the same time, Holiday said: "Do you want to get coffee together soon?"

"Oh. OK."

Holiday looked at me strangely. "But only if you want to."

"No, that sounds great," I lied. It did not sound great. It sounded boring.

"Great!" said Holiday.

"Who was that?" Jasper asked when I came back to the group.

"Someone from home," I said.

"Was she your girlfriend?" Jasper asked with a grin.

"No! Our moms are friends."

"OK," said Jasper. "Sit down. We're playing Lies."

"How do we play?" I asked. "Do you just have to lie?"

"Yes," said Eliza. "The best lie wins."

"I'll start," said Doc. "Linden works at a burger restaurant!"

Everyone laughed, and I did too, but I felt **embarrassed**. Doc was close to the truth, but he didn't know it.

"I've got one," Jasper said suddenly. He turned to Meredith and grinned. "Meredith's boyfriend is **cheating** on her. But she's too stupid to understand that he doesn't love her."

Everyone went quiet.

"Oh, sorry," said Jasper. He grinned at Meredith. "I forgot that I was supposed to lie."

But Meredith didn't laugh. Nobody did.

"You're horrible!" Meredith said. She jumped up and ran across the beach.

"Yeah?" shouted Jasper. "You're even worse!"

"Why do you have to be like this?" asked Eliza, angrily. "Meredith didn't do anything wrong."

"She's dating Greg, and then she comes to our house and eats our food," said Jasper.

"Meredith was right," said Eliza. "You *are* horrible." She turned and walked across the beach to find Meredith.

———

I found Eliza sitting on the beach away from the party.

"Where's Meredith?" I asked.

"She left," said Eliza quietly. "Did you know that we all used to be good friends? Us, Meredith, and Greg. Our parents, too. I wanted it to always be like that. Was that stupid of me?"

"No," I said.

"This is because of Greg's dad," Eliza said. "Everything that happened last year is because of him."

I didn't reply. I didn't want Eliza to know that Jasper didn't talk to me about their family and their problems.

"Dad had some money problems," said Eliza, "and Greg's dad learned about it. He told the police, and our dad went to jail for ten months."

Jail?

"That's terrible," I said.

Why didn't Jasper tell me? But I couldn't be angry at Jasper, because I had big secrets too.

"Yeah," said Eliza. "And Greg didn't even act

like he was sorry. He became horrible, and so did my brother."

"And now Jasper doesn't like Meredith," I said. "Because she's dating Greg."

"Yes. I just want us all to be friends again," said Eliza. Then, she smiled at me. "Sorry. This is your vacation. You don't want to hear about all my stupid rich girl's problems."

I wanted to say, "I want to hear everything that you have to say about it," but I didn't. I didn't ask her anything more — and maybe that was a mistake.

Jasper woke me up in the morning. "I want to go into town and get some food for later," he said.

After breakfast we went to a small store. When Jasper went to find his favorite — and very expensive — food, I saw the waitress from Red's. She was shopping there, too.

"Hey!" I said.

". . . Hi."

"Last night," I said. "At the restaurant."

"Yes, I remember," she said.

I wanted to say, "Sorry about Meredith. It was

very rude of her," but I didn't.

"Linden!" Jasper shouted, suddenly. Then, he saw the waitress and smiled at her. "Hey! Sorry Meredith was so rude last night. My parents are leaving the island to see some friends tonight, so we're having a party at August House. Do you want to come?"

"Maybe."

"This is my friend, Linden. Linden, this is Aidy. Aidy, will you come tonight or not?"

Aidy smiled. "I'll come."

We left the store, and I said to Jasper, "I didn't know that you knew her."

"I like Aidy," he said. "I wanted to date her, but I told Greg, and then he kissed her."

"Does Meredith know?"

"I think that she does," Jasper said. "She was very rude to Aidy last night."

"I don't think that she'll be happy to see Aidy at the party."

Jasper laughed. "It's my house. I don't care about Meredith's feelings."

CHAPTER THREE
The fight

The garden was full of people laughing and drinking. But Eliza wasn't with them.

I found her in the library with a book at around 11:30 p.m. "What are you doing here?" I asked.

"I don't like parties," she said. "Let's go outside."

I followed her to a quiet part of the garden. "Can I ask a question about you and Doc?" I said.

Eliza grinned. "Are you jealous?"

"Yeah," I laughed. "A little bit."

"Don't be jealous. We're just friends. Anyway, there's another person I like."

I smiled at her. "OK."

I wanted to kiss her, but then Eliza saw someone behind me. "What is *he* doing here?"

I turned around and saw Jasper push past Meredith. He stood next to Wells near the garden door. Wells was looking at a boy.

"Who is that?" I thought.

"Can't you stay on your own beach, Greg?" Jasper said, angrily, to the boy.

Greg. It was Meredith's boyfriend. He was tall

THE FIGHT

with strong arms, and he was wearing a baseball cap. He did not look worried or angry.

"Go back to your own beach," said Wells.

"Stop," said Jasper. He put a hand on Wells's arm. "Greg is leaving now. He doesn't want to start a fight."

Greg laughed. "You couldn't fight me."

I agreed. He was bigger than Wells and Jasper.

Wells took a step closer to Greg and opened his mouth, but Jasper quickly said, "No, Wells."

"Stop it, Jasper!" Wells shouted. "Are you Greg's friend, or are you my brother?"

"Shut up, Wells!" said Jasper.

Greg grinned. "Yeah. *Shut up, Wells.*"

That was when Wells hit Greg in the face. Jasper tried to pull Wells away from Greg, and I pushed in to help him.

"Get your hands off me, Linden," Wells shouted. He pushed me away, and then he hit Greg again. Greg hit him back hard.

Doc ran to help me and Jasper. Together we pulled Wells away from Greg.

"Are you OK?" Meredith asked. She tried to touch Greg's arm, but he stepped away.

"Get out of here," said Jasper.

"Fine," said Greg, and he started to walk away. He looked at Meredith, but she did not follow him.

"OK," Eliza said when Greg was gone. "Everyone needs to leave. Now."

I started to help Jasper clean the garden and pool. Wells was not there.

"What happened to your brother?" I asked.

Jasper laughed. "Wells never helps to clean."

It was one in the morning when we finished cleaning. I went upstairs, but I stopped in front of Eliza's bedroom door.

"Don't be afraid," I said to myself. "Just do it."

I **knocked** on her door.

THE FIGHT

I woke up to the sound of someone screaming.

"Where am I?" I thought. "Mom? Is that her screaming? Is she OK?"

Then, I remembered that I was staying with Jasper. Eliza was outside, screaming. I jumped out of bed and ran downstairs. It was still dark, but there were bright lights by the pool.

Eliza was standing in front of it. There was a man's body in the pool. Half of his body was on the steps, and the other half was still in the water. There was **blood** on the back of his head.

"Linden!" Wells ran out of the door. "Help me."

I ran to Wells. We pulled out the body and turned it over.

"It's Greg," said Wells. "What's he doing here?"

"Is he dead?" asked Eliza. She sounded afraid.

"I don't know," said Wells. "We need to call the police."

Eliza ran inside the house to get her phone.

"What's happening?" Jasper said suddenly. He stepped out into the garden with Aidy. Meredith ran out behind them. They all stopped when they saw Greg's body. Then, Meredith started screaming.

Everything happened quickly after that. The police arrived with an ambulance. Greg wasn't dead, but he needed help quickly. The ambulance took him to the hospital, and Meredith followed it.

Two police officers called Reyes and O'Neal stayed at the house to ask us questions.

"What happened here?" asked Reyes.

"Greg is our friend," said Wells. "He came to our party last night, but he went home early. I don't know what he did after that."

"What other people were here last night?" asked O'Neal.

"No one," said Eliza. "It was just us and

Meredith. She's Greg's girlfriend."

"Why are they lying?" I thought. There were a lot of people at the party last night. I looked at Eliza, Jasper, and Aidy.

"Are they going to tell the police about the fight?" I thought. But they didn't say anything.

"Is Greg OK?" asked Eliza.

Reyes looked at O'Neal, and then he said, "Greg is in a **coma**."

———

"Should I go home?" I asked Jasper after lunch.

Jasper looked at me in surprise. "What? Why?"

It was strange. Everyone was acting normally. Why didn't they care? Even the police didn't ask many questions about Greg or us.

"Don't worry about Greg," said Jasper. "He's going to be fine."

"How do you know?" I said.

Jasper didn't answer my question. He just said, "Come to the beach with us."

"You're really going to the beach?" It didn't feel good to go there when Greg was in the hospital, but I didn't want to say more. So I just said, "OK."

"Get your things, and meet us down there,"

said Jasper, and then he walked down the stairs to the beach.

I started to walk to my room, but I saw something in the pool. I took it out of the water and looked at it. It was a **broken** necklace.

"Whose necklace is this?" I thought.

I walked into the house and saw Eliza in the kitchen. "Are you coming to the beach with us?" she asked.

"Yes," I said, deciding not to tell her about the necklace. "I just need to get my things."

"Good." Eliza smiled at me.

"Can I ask you something?" I said. "What were you doing outside so early this morning?"

Eliza looked surprised. "Whimsy wanted to go outside, so I went to open the door for her. Why?"

"I just wanted to know," I said. But I didn't remember seeing Whimsy in the garden. "I'm going to my room now. I'll see you later."

When I got to my room, I looked at my phone. I had a message from Holiday. It said: "Hi! Do you still want to get coffee today?"

I messaged her back and said: "Where shall I meet you?"

CHAPTER FOUR
Suspects

"Wow," said Holiday. We were at a coffee shop. "Do you think somebody tried to kill Greg?"

"What? No! I didn't say that!"

"Nobody liked Greg. You found him in the swimming pool, and now he's in a coma. What do you think happened?"

"I don't think anything!" I said. "It was an **accident**."

I forgot that Holiday loved **mysteries**. But now she thought that someone tried to kill Greg. I didn't like that. She was **accusing** my friends of doing something terrible.

But wasn't I thinking the same thing?

"OK," said Holiday, slowly. "Well, I'm happy that you messaged me. I didn't think that you were happy to see me on the beach."

"No," I said quickly. "I *was* happy to see you."

"Are you sure?"

"Yes," I said. "But I know all these people from school, and none of them know that I have a scholarship."

"Did you think that I was going to walk up to your friends and say 'Hello! Did you know that Linden is working class?'" asked Holiday.

"You don't understand," I said angrily. "It's hard when you're different from everyone."

Everyone on the island was rich, and so was Holiday. My life was different, and Holiday didn't understand that.

Holiday was quiet for a minute, and then she said, "Does your leg still hurt?"

I was surprised that she knew about the crash. I wanted to lie. But I said, "Yes. It hurts a lot."

Holiday gave me a small smile. "OK. Let's think about last night. Do you think that it was really an accident? Maybe someone wanted to hurt Greg?"

"Nobody wanted to hurt Greg," I said, quickly.

"**Liar**," said Holiday.

"This isn't one of your mystery books, Holiday. These are my friends. I can't just start accusing and **investigating** them."

"I'm not asking you to accuse or investigate them," said Holiday. "I just want you to think."

"I think they all wanted to hurt him," I said.

Holiday pulled a piece of paper and a pen out of her bag. "Tell me everything that happened."

I told Holiday the story of last night. We sat there in the coffee shop all afternoon. Holiday wrote down everything I said and asked me a lot of questions.

I started to feel silly while I answered them. I was sad about Greg, but it was an accident.

"Where was Greg's body when you found him?"

"Half of his body was on the steps, and the other half was in the water," I replied. "And there was blood on the back of his head."

Holiday was quiet for a moment, and then she said, "I think that someone moved his body."

"Why do you think that?"

"If Greg fell into the pool, then the blood should be on the front of his head. But it's on the back. How did that happen?"

"I don't know!" I shouted.

"Let's talk about **suspects**," said Holiday.

"Maybe Wells is a suspect," I said. "Wells and Greg had a fight. And Wells doesn't like Greg."

"Why not?" asked Holiday.

"Because their dads had some trouble with the law last year," I said.

"Then Eliza and Jasper must be suspects too," said Holiday.

"I know Jasper well," I said. "He didn't hurt Greg."

Jasper didn't like to fight, and Greg was much bigger than him. I knew that Jasper didn't push Greg into the pool.

"OK," said Holiday. "What about Eliza?"

"Eliza didn't do it," I said quickly. "She has an **alibi**."

"Really?" said Holiday. "And who is her alibi?"

I was her alibi. I knocked on Eliza's door and stayed in her room until 3 a.m. We kissed and talked about life and the party, and then we slept. I woke up and left because I didn't want Jasper or Wells to see me in Eliza's room. But I didn't want to tell Holiday that.

"It doesn't matter," I said. "But Eliza didn't do it."

"OK," said Holiday. She didn't look like she **believed** me. "Can you show me the necklace?"

I put it in her hand.

"It's an expensive necklace," she said. "A lot of rich girls on the island wear these necklaces."

Eliza was a rich girl.

"Anyway," said Holiday. She put the necklace in her bag. "I think that we should talk to our suspects."

"No!" I said.

"Michael," said Holiday. "You told me everything because you think that something strange happened to Greg. You don't believe that it was an accident."

This was true. I didn't want to accuse my friends of hurting Greg, but something was wrong.

"You're right," I said.

"I usually am," said Holiday.

I looked at my phone. I had a message from Jasper. It said: *Where are you?*

"I have to go back to August House," I said.

"I have to go home, too," said Holiday. "Shall I

take you back in my car?"

"No, thanks." I walked out of the coffee shop, and Holiday followed me. "Do you want to come over to August House tonight?" I asked. "I'll message you later."

"OK," she said, but I don't think that she believed me. I didn't even believe me. "See you, Linden." She started to walk away.

"Holiday!" I shouted.

Holiday turned and looked at me.

"I just wanted to say thank you. I was very worried this morning." I said.

Holiday smiled. "You don't have to thank me. We're friends."

CHAPTER FIVE
The sweater

Greg was still in a coma.

Meredith came back to August House while we were watching TV. Her face was white, and she was still wearing the same clothes from the morning. She looked terrible. Eliza and Meredith went upstairs to talk, and when Eliza came back down, I said, "How is she?"

"Not good," said Eliza. "Greg is very sick."

"Did the police or doctors say anything to her?" I asked. "Do they have any ideas?"

Eliza looked at me strangely. "Not really. Meredith just said he was only in the water for one hour."

I thought about Holiday and our meeting today. Holiday thought that Eliza was a suspect, but I couldn't believe that.

I messaged Holiday later, and she came to August House while we were finishing our dinner in the garden.

"Hey," she said as she looked around at all of us. She was wearing different clothes from this afternoon, and her curly hair was down her back.

She looked pretty, and I knew that Wells thought the same.

"This is Holiday," I said. "She's my friend from home."

"Hey," said Wells. I didn't like the way that he looked at her. "Come and sit with us."

"Oh!" said Eliza suddenly. She smiled at Holiday. "I know you! I saw you at the music store on the island. You were buying a CD."

Meredith, Eliza, and Holiday began to talk and laugh together. They knew some of the same rich girls from Martha's Vineyard.

"What was Linden like as a little boy?" Wells asked suddenly. "Tell us something **embarrassing** about him."

My face started to feel warm. Holiday and I were children together, and I knew that she had many embarrassing stories about me.

But she just laughed and said nothing.

"Thank you, Holiday," I thought.

Then, Eliza and Holiday started to play a game. Jasper and Wells jumped into the pool. Meredith sat quietly on a chair. Nobody said anything about Greg.

"Maybe I should stop thinking about him," I thought.

Then, Meredith stood up and walked into the kitchen. Holiday looked at me, and she stood up, too.

"Where's the bathroom?" she asked Eliza.

"I'll show you," I said. I stood up, and we walked into the kitchen together.

"Meredith!" Holiday said loudly. "Is this yours?" She showed Meredith the broken necklace.

Meredith looked surprised. "Oh, yeah, it is. Thank you. Aidy pulled it off my neck."

"Jasper's Aidy?" I said loudly.

Meredith laughed, but it wasn't a nice laugh. "That girl doesn't like Jasper. She just likes money. She's dated every rich boy on this island." Meredith suddenly pointed at her neck. "Did you know that she **scratched** me with her **nails** last night? Look at my neck."

There were three red **scratches** on Meredith's neck.

"Oh no," said Holiday. She looked at Meredith kindly. It was the way that you look at a good friend. "Did you two fight about something?"

"Greg kissed Aidy at the beginning of summer," Meredith said. "And now she thinks that Greg wants to date her, but he doesn't. He only wants to date me."

"Do you think that . . ." I started to ask.

Meredith laughed loudly. "Do I think that Aidy pushed Greg into the pool? I don't like her but no, I don't think that she pushed Greg. Aidy was with Jasper all night. I could hear them in his bedroom."

I looked at Holiday. Was she thinking the same thing as me?

Aidy had an alibi, but was Meredith a suspect now too?

———

Holiday and I went to Red's the next afternoon. Holiday knew that Aidy was working there.

"Hi Linden," said Aidy when she saw me. Her hair was pulled up, and she had white paint on her short nails. "Who is this?"

"This is my friend, Holiday. We wanted to ask you . . ."

But then Holiday kicked me under the table and said, "Can we have two colas, please?"

"OK," said Aidy, and she walked away to get our drinks.

When she was gone, Holiday turned to look at me. She didn't look happy. "Don't be stupid, Michael. You can't just ask her about Meredith and Greg or she'll know that she's a suspect. We have to be nice to her and ask different questions first."

When Aidy came back with our drinks, I said, "Did you see the fight with Greg, Jasper, and Wells the other night? Wasn't it crazy?"

Aidy looked at me, and then she looked at Holiday. "Is it true that Greg is in a coma?"

"Yes," I said. "Is it true that you kissed Greg?"

"Did Meredith tell you that?" Aidy asked. She didn't look happy. "What other things did she tell you?"

"We know about your fight with Meredith," I said. "You pulled off her necklace."

"I really don't like that girl," said Aidy. "I didn't know that Greg had a girlfriend when I kissed him!"

"*Did* you pull off her necklace?" I asked.

"Yes," said Aidy, and she grinned. "But those necklaces are ugly anyway."

Holiday smiled. "You're right."

Holiday was very good at **pretending** to be friends with people. She did the same thing to Meredith the night before.

"Can I tell you something?" said Aidy. "I think that Meredith pushed Greg in the pool."

"Really?" I said.

"No, not really," laughed Aidy. "I don't like her, but she's not a killer. And she has an alibi."

"Does she?" asked Holiday. "Who?"

"Me," said Aidy. "I stayed in Jasper's room that night. I went to the bathroom at 4 a.m., and I saw Meredith. Her bedroom door was open. She was sleeping." Aidy stepped away from our table and waved. "I have to get back to work now. Bye."

When we were **alone** again, Holiday smiled at me. "You asked some good questions, Michael."

"Do you think that Aidy is telling the truth?" I asked.

"I don't know," said Holiday. "But if Greg was only in the water for one hour, then Meredith didn't push him."

"That's right," I said. "Because Aidy saw her

sleeping at 4 a.m."

"I think that we need to look at a new suspect," said Holiday.

"Who?" I asked.

Holiday smiled. "Wells. He **disappeared** after the party. Where did he go?"

"I don't know," I said.

"Tell me everything again," said Holiday. "What was Greg wearing in the pool?"

"Red shorts," I said.

"Was he wearing a shirt?" asked Holiday.

"No," I said.

"Was he wearing a shirt at the party?"

"Yes," I said. "Or maybe he was wearing a sweater. I don't remember."

"OK," said Holiday. "We need to check Wells's room."

August House was quiet when we got back. Mrs. Kendrick was sitting by the pool, Mr. Kendrick was in his office, and Jasper and the others were down at the beach.

Wells's room was at the end of the hall. I put my hand on the door then stopped. I didn't want to go into his room, but I had too many questions. What happened to Greg? Who pushed him?

I opened the door.

"What are we looking for?" I asked Holiday.

"I don't know," said Holiday. "Just keep looking. When we see it, we'll know."

We started to look around, but we didn't find anything. Suddenly, I heard feet on the stairs.

"Oh no," I thought. "Someone is coming." I pulled Holiday behind Wells's bedroom door. She was standing very close to me.

"Be quiet," I said.

We waited until we couldn't hear the noise outside any more, and then Holiday stepped away from me.

"Can we get out of here now?" I said.

"No," Holiday said. She started looking under Wells's bed, and then she stood up and grinned at me. She was holding something. "Look!"

It was a sweater, and there were some letters on it. The letters said: *GTH*. And next to the letters, there was blood.

"Was Greg wearing this at the party?" asked Holiday.

"Maybe," I said. "Why is it in here? Did Wells take it off Greg after he pushed him into the pool?"

"I don't think that he did that," said Holiday. "But Wells will be a suspect if the police find it."

"I don't know," I said. "Wells is stupid. He doesn't think about things like that. We need to get out of his room now."

"OK," said Holiday. She put the sweater back under Wells's bed. "Let's go."

CHAPTER SIX
Wells's secret

There was a big street party on the island that night. Everyone was going into town to enjoy it. Holiday and I agreed to meet in town so that we could watch Wells.

Mr. Kendrick drove us there. He asked me a lot of questions about lacrosse, but I didn't want to answer them because my leg was still hurting me.

Jasper went to find Aidy as soon as we got into town, and I started looking for Holiday. But I couldn't find her. That made me happy because I wanted to be with Eliza. I met her sitting alone on a wall and wearing a short dress. She looked beautiful and I wanted to kiss her.

I sat down next to her and said, "Do you want to get out of here and go for a walk with me?"

Eliza grinned at me. "Yes please!"

We walked to a quiet part of the town away from the party.

"You hate parties," I said. "Why did you come tonight?"

"It makes my parents happy. I wanted to do

something nice for my family after . . ." said Eliza.

I knew that she was talking about her dad being in jail.

"Anyway," Eliza said. She smiled at me, but now she looked a little sad. "I'm happy that you're here with me."

I was trying to think of something to say to that, but then I saw Holiday. She was running across the road to me and Eliza.

"There you are, Linden. I was looking for you," said Holiday. "Can you come with me? I need your help."

I didn't move. I knew that Holiday still wanted

to investigate Wells, but I was enjoying my time with Eliza. "Do you really need me this minute?" I asked.

Holiday looked angry for a second, but only I saw it. Then, she smiled. "No, it's OK. I can do it alone."

Now I felt like an **asshole**. "No, I'll come with you," I said. "Sorry, Eliza. I'll come back soon."

"It's fine," said Eliza, but I didn't believe her. But how could I say, "I do really want to know you, but I believe that your brother tried to murder someone, and we need to investigate him"?

Eliza walked away, and I was alone with Holiday. "What do you want to do?" I said.

Holiday knew that I wasn't happy, and I waited for her to shout at me, but she just pointed across the street.

"Look at them," she said.

Wells was there standing next to a blue car and talking to an older woman.

"Who's she?" I asked Holiday.

Holiday looked at me like I was stupid. "That's Greg's mom."

"Oh wow," I said. "Why isn't she at the hospital with Greg?"

"Greg has a little sister," said Holiday. "Maybe they came here to make things normal for her."

"Maybe," I said, but Wells was standing very close to Greg's mom and their hands were touching. "Do you think that they're . . . ?"

"*Dating*? Yes," said Holiday. "Isn't it terrible? How old is Wells?"

"He's twenty," I said. "So in law it's OK for them to date, but it's horrible."

"Do you think that Greg knew about them?"

asked Holiday. "Maybe he saw them kissing."

"Maybe he and Wells had another fight about it, and Wells pushed Greg in the pool," I said.

"We need to investigate more," said Holiday. "Meet me at the beach near Greg's house tomorrow morning."

Holiday was wearing running shorts and shoes the next morning.

"Why are you wearing that?" I asked her. "Are we going running?"

"No," said Holiday.

"Why are you wearing those clothes then?" I asked.

"Because Greg's mom must think that I'm a runner. I'm going to knock on the door now. You stay here."

Holiday starting running to Greg's door, and his mom opened it. I didn't want her to see me, so I stood behind a tree.

"Hello," said Greg's mom to Holiday. "Can I help you?"

Holiday pretended to cry. "Have you seen my dog? Her name is Bunny. I was taking her for a run on the beach, but she's disappeared."

"Oh no," said Greg's mom. "I'm sorry."

"Can I use your phone?" asked Holiday. "I need to tell my mom, and I left my phone at home."

"OK," said Greg's mom. She gave Holiday her phone.

"Thank you," said Holiday. "I'll bring it back soon."

Holiday walked away from Greg's house and pretended to speak on the phone. "Mom?" she said, loudly, as she walked back to the tree. "I lost the dog on the beach!"

"You're good at pretending," I said when she stopped in front of the tree.

"I know," said Holiday. Then, she showed me Greg's mom's phone. "We have to look through this quickly."

"What?" I said. "Why?"

"I still think that someone pushed Greg into the pool," said Holiday. "But it wasn't Wells. Look at this."

I looked at the phone. Greg's family had a **security** camera for their home and Greg's mom could watch the videos on her phone. Holiday showed me a video from the night of the party.

It was 1 a.m. in the video and Wells was standing

outside Greg's mom's door.

"It doesn't mean that Wells isn't a suspect," I said to Holiday. "Maybe he went back to August House later and saw Greg."

"I thought of that, but look at the security camera video," said Holiday. "It **proves** that Wells stayed with Greg's mom until 4.30 a.m."

I looked at the video again. The time on the video showed 4.30 a.m. Wells was standing outside the house and he was kissing Greg's mom.

"Look!" I said. "He's wearing the sweater."

Holiday pulled the phone away from me. "This proves that Wells is **innocent**. He didn't push Greg into the pool."

"But why did the sweater have Greg's blood on it?" I asked.

"It wasn't Greg's blood," said Holiday. "It was Wells's blood. He got hurt from the fight at the party. Then, he came to Greg's house and stayed for a few hours. Greg's mom gave him one of Greg's sweaters to wear."

"Oh," I said, feeling really bad now. If Holiday was right, then Wells really was innocent.

Holiday walked back to the house and gave the phone to Greg's mom.

"We need to stop investigating this," I said to Holiday. "I don't want to accuse my friends any more. This isn't a mystery. It was just an accident. But we can still meet. I'm here for a few more days."

"OK. I think I'll go home now," Holiday answered, and her voice was not angry or happy.

But when she left, I felt strangely sad.

When I got back to August House, I saw Eliza sitting next to the pool. I smiled at her and said, "Hey. Do you want to get something to eat with me tonight?"

Eliza smiled back at me. "We could do that," she said. "But I don't want to have dinner with a rude person. Maybe I'll go to the beach with Doc." Then, she stood up and walked away.

Jasper laughed at me. "Eliza thinks that you're an asshole."

"She's not wrong," I said, and jumped into the pool.

CHAPTER SEVEN
Topher

Holiday and I didn't talk for days. But I didn't think about her. I was trying to become friends with Eliza again. "I'm sorry that I was an asshole last night," I told her. "Holiday is just a friend. We had things to do but that's finished now."

A few days later, Eliza and I were swimming in the pool. "I have to leave tomorrow," I said.

Eliza looked at me and then she said, "Come with me."

She took me up to the top of August House, and we opened a window and looked outside.

"The **view** is beautiful here," said Eliza.

I smiled. "Yes, the view is beautiful."

Eliza laughed. "You're trying too hard, Linden. But I'll pretend that I think it's sweet because I like you."

I liked Eliza, too, but I started to think about Greer. I liked Greer a lot and everything ended badly with her.

"Do you have to leave?" Eliza asked. "A **hurricane** will hit the island in the next two days."

I didn't understand. "Don't people usually leave the island when a hurricane is coming?"

"Not my family," said Eliza with a grin. "We usually close the windows and doors, buy lots of food, and have a party. You should stay."

I was sitting in the garden with Jasper, Eliza, and Aidy later that night, and Jasper said the same thing. "Stay for a few more days. It's nice having you here."

"OK," I said. "I'll stay."

Eliza smiled at me. "Good." And then she said, "I want to smoke some **weed**. Do you have anything, Jasper?"

"No," said Jasper. "We finished everything."

"Go and buy some more," said Eliza.

"I don't want to," said Jasper. "Greg has weed, but I don't like him."

"Do you have anything, Aidy?" asked Eliza.

"Why are you asking me?" she answered angrily. "Do you think that I have weed just because I'm not rich?"

"No!" said Eliza. She looked embarrassed. "Greg is rich, and he always has weed. He sells it too — for someone in Boston."

"I must tell Holiday that," I thought. I didn't

want to investigate any more, but now I knew that Greg sold weed.

I took one of the Kendricks' bikes and rode to Holiday's house.

She opened the door for me, and she looked surprised. "Michael? What are you doing here?"

"I'm sorry," I said. "You were right. We need to keep investigating."

"Why?" Holiday asked.

"Greg sells weed for someone in Boston," I told her. "I don't know their name, but they must be a suspect."

"I think that you're right," said Holiday. "The security camera video from Greg's house proved that Wells is innocent, but I saw another person in the video."

"Who did you see?" I asked.

"A red car stopped outside Greg's house about an hour before the party at August House. A man got out of the car, Greg came out of the house, and the man started shouting. I paid someone to **research** the car, and it's owned by a man called Topher. He sells weed."

"Do you think that Greg was selling weed on the island for Topher?" I asked.

"Yes," said Holiday. "Maybe Greg **owes** Topher money. I don't know, but I think that we need to investigate Topher."

I tried not to smile, but it was hard.

Holiday drove us to the hospital. "We need to find Topher, and I think that he'll come there."

"Why?" I asked.

"Greg owes him money," Holiday said. "Topher needs that money before he goes back to Boston."

"I don't think that he will come to the hospital," I said, "because Greg is in a coma."

But Holiday was right. We waited outside the hospital for a short while, and we talked and laughed like we were more than friends.

Holiday looked at me, and her face was turning red. I sat up and looked away.

"What is wrong with me?" I thought. "Why am I talking to Holiday like this?"

"That's the car!" she said suddenly. "There he is!" We both watched as a tall man climbed out of a red car and walked into the hospital. Two minutes later, he came out and started to drive away.

"We need to follow him," said Holiday.

We followed Topher to a small and cheap hotel, but he didn't get out of his car.

"What's he doing?" I asked.

"I don't know," said Holiday.

Suddenly, the car door opened, and Topher climbed out. He looked straight at us.

"Oh no," said Holiday. She looked afraid.

Topher walked to our car and knocked on the window. "Open it," he said.

Holiday opened the window.

"Who are you working for?" Topher asked angrily. "I saw you at the hospital. Why are you following me?"

"We're not following you!" said Holiday. "We just wanted to be alone together."

I forgot that Holiday was a very good liar. I don't know if Topher believed her, but he said, "Just get out of here. And if I see you two again, I'm going to kill you."

We started the car and didn't stop driving until we were outside August House.

"I think that we should tell the police about Topher," I said.

"No," said Holiday. "If we tell the police about Topher, he'll just disappear. We're so close to **solving** this mystery, Michael, I can feel it. Can you feel it?"

I looked at her curly hair and wide eyes, her full smiling mouth. "Yeah," I said softly. "I can feel it."

And just for a second, I thought about . . .

"Michael," Holiday said.

"Yeah," I said. "What shall we do next?"

"Topher's hotel had security cameras," said Holiday. "We need to check the video and see if Topher has an alibi for the night of the party."

We borrowed one of the Kendricks' cars and drove back to the hotel the next day. We drove up and down the road, until we were sure that Topher's car wasn't there.

"How are we going to look at the video?" I asked, as we walked to the hotel's security office.

Holiday showed me her bag. There was money inside. "I'm going to **bribe** the man in the security office."

There was only one person in the office. "I don't think that I should do this," he said.

Holiday pushed the **bribe** money to him. "I won't tell anyone," she said. "But he's my boyfriend. I need to know if he's cheating on me."

The man looked at the money. "My girlfriend cheated on me last year," he said sadly, and then he took it. "OK," he said. "But be quick."

He showed us the security camera video from the night of the party. Topher arrived at the hotel at about 1.30 a.m. in his red car. We knew that Greg wasn't in the pool at that time.

"Maybe he comes out again?" I asked. "Can you show us some more?"

"OK," said the security man.

We watched more of the video, but Topher didn't come out of the hotel until 11 a.m.

I looked at Holiday. We knew that we were thinking the same thing: Topher was innocent.

CHAPTER EIGHT
Hurricane party

"Wells is innocent. Topher is innocent. Was it just an accident?" I asked Holiday as we drove back to August House. "Maybe Greg did fall into the pool."

"Maybe," said Holiday, but it didn't sound like she believed me.

I was getting tired of our investigating. It was my last night at August House and tonight was the hurricane party. I just wanted to have fun.

I stopped the car outside Holiday's house. Then, she said, "Do you still want me to come to the hurricane party?"

I told her about the party a few days ago. I didn't want her to come now, but I said "Yes, of course. 8 p.m.?"

Holiday smiled. "I'll be there."

When I walked inside August House, everyone was getting ready for the hurricane. Aidy and Jasper were putting food on the table. Wells was playing music. And Eliza and Doc were playing a game together. Everyone looked happy and excited, and I knew that I should feel excited too. But I didn't.

I felt worried. The storm was arriving, and it was raining hard. I felt that something bad was going to happen.

When Holiday arrived that evening, she was acting strangely. I pulled her into the library and closed the door. "What's wrong with you tonight?" I asked her.

"I need to talk to you about Eliza," she said. "I don't think her alibi is true."

"I'm her alibi!" I said.

"You weren't together all night," said Holiday. "And I learned something about Eliza earlier. Did you know that she had to leave her boarding school?"

"Yes, I did," I said.

"Do you know why she left?" asked Holiday.

"No," I said.

"Do you remember that Eliza and I know some of the same girls? Well, I phoned one of them. A girl at Eliza's school fell from her horse," said Holiday. "Eliza didn't like her. It was a bad accident, and the girl had to go to hospital."

"Do you think the accident was because of Eliza?" I asked.

"I don't know," said Holiday. "But the school thought that it was. Eliza left soon after the accident."

"I don't believe you," I said. "You just don't like Eliza."

Holiday looked surprised. "I do like Eliza! But she's a suspect. First there was an accident with the girl at her school, and now the accident with Greg."

"You're jealous because I like Eliza!"

I knew that wasn't the right thing to say to Holiday, but it was too late.

"You think that I want to date you?" she said, angrily. "I don't even like you, Michael. You're **obsessed** with rich people. Why did I come here? I should go."

Suddenly the lights went out, and we could hear the rain and the wind outside.

"It's too dangerous to leave now," I said. "The hurricane has started."

Holiday didn't look happy about that. "Fine," she said, "then let's not talk any more. We did it for years and we can do it again."

I found Eliza in the kitchen, and I smiled at her.

"Are you enjoying the party?" she asked.

"No," I said. "Are you?"

Eliza didn't answer my question. She said, "Let's go to my room."

I knew that Holiday was watching while I followed Eliza upstairs. "Good," I thought. "I hope that she's jealous."

Eliza closed her bedroom door. "I like you, Linden," she said.

"I like you, too," I said. And then we sat down on her bed, and I kissed her.

Eliza smiled at me after we finished. "Everything feels good again for the first time this summer. I'm not even worried about Greg any more."

"Why?" I asked.

"I think that he **deserved** to fall into the pool," said Eliza. "Greg isn't a good person."

But I was starting to think that *Eliza* wasn't a good person.

"I'll be back," said Eliza. She looked quickly at her phone, then stood up and walked into the bathroom.

I looked at her phone. It was a terrible thing, but the phone was still open, and I had to move quickly. I picked it up.

Eliza sent one message to Greg on the night of the party. It said: *Stay away from my family, or you'll **regret** it.*

Holiday was right. Eliza pushed Greg into the pool. My **obsession** with her stopped me seeing the truth before.

I heard the bathroom door open, and I quickly put down her phone. "Let's go downstairs," I said, and I began putting on my clothes.

Eliza looked at me strangely. "Are you OK?"

"Yes," I said, and I tried to smile. "Let's go."

When we came downstairs, I heard Wells talking about Greg.

"I don't know what happened," Wells said. "But he deserved it."

Jasper, Eliza, Aidy, and Doc all started laughing. I couldn't believe it. They were horrible people.

"That's enough!" I shouted. "Greg's in a coma. Do you think that's funny?" I turned to look at Wells. "Do you think that dating Greg's mom is funny too, Wells?"

Everyone went quiet. Jasper turned to look at Wells.

"I'm sorry?" he said.

"You are dating Helene Holliman?" Eliza asked, and she sounded really surprised.

"Shut up, Linden," said Wells. "You're a liar."

"No, I'm not," I said.

"Michael," Holiday said suddenly. "Don't do this."

But I needed to say it. "And Eliza pushed Greg in the pool!"

Everyone turned to look at me.

"I read your message to Greg," I told Eliza.

"You said 'Stay away from my family, or you'll regret it'. You didn't wake up early to open the door for Whimsy. You were in the garden, because you pushed Greg!"

The room was quiet, and then Doc said, "Eliza was at my house that night. She woke up, and you weren't there, so she came to my house."

I couldn't believe it. "Why?"

"I wanted to talk about my family problems," said Eliza. "I wanted to talk to you about them, but you weren't there! Then, I came back from Doc's and found Greg in the pool. I couldn't tell you that I was at Doc's, because you were jealous of him."

"No," I said. "You pushed Greg into the pool. You're a bad person. You had to leave your old school, because you hurt a girl."

"I left my school because I was sad about my family!" Eliza shouted.

"You're the worst person, Linden," said Wells.

"You're so obsessed with money," said Eliza. "You think that everyone is trying to win a game. But the only person in the game is you."

I didn't know what to say, but I didn't have to say anything, because Meredith suddenly walked into the room. She was crying and her hair was wet with rain. "Greg is dead," she said, then she disappeared up the stairs.

CHAPTER NINE
The truth

As soon as the hurricane finished, I packed and went to catch the boat to Boston. But Holiday found me.

"Wait, Michael," she said. "You can't leave."

"I don't want to be here any more, Holiday," I said. "I know that you and everyone at August House must hate me."

"Maybe they do hate you," said Holiday. "But we're friends, and I solved the mystery. I know who pushed Greg into the pool."

"Who did it?" I asked.

Holiday grinned at me. "Come with me."

"OK," I said, and I got into her car.

"How did you solve it?" I asked Holiday as she stopped outside August House. Meredith was sitting outside with a big bag.

"Are you leaving?" Holiday asked her.

"Yes," said Meredith. She was still crying.

Holiday smiled at Meredith. "Please stop

pretending to cry."

"What?" said Meredith.

The front door opened and I saw Wells, Aidy, Jasper, and Eliza standing in the hall. Holiday quickly started to speak again.

"We know that Greg owed Topher money for selling his weed, but Greg didn't have the money any more. Why? Did someone steal it?" Holiday pointed at Meredith. "Didn't your parents sell their house on the island?"

"Yes," said Meredith. "This island is so boring."

"I don't think they sold their house because the island is boring," said Holiday. "They sold it because they had money problems. Your family lost their money, but you still had enough money to buy an expensive necklace," said Holiday. "You stole the money from Greg."

Everyone was quiet.

"You told us that Aidy scratched your neck at the party," said Holiday. "But Aidy has short nails. Somebody scratched you, but it wasn't Aidy. Why did Aidy lie for you?"

"It was an accident!" Aidy said suddenly.

"Shut up!" said Meredith.

"No!" said Aidy. "I was just trying to help you.

But I can't do this any more. Not now that he's dead."

"What *really* happened that night?" asked Holiday.

Aidy looked at Jasper. "I got up early to go home. I didn't regret it, but I didn't want it to be strange with you in the morning. That's when I saw Greg and Meredith fighting. Greg knew that Meredith stole his money. He pushed Meredith hard. I don't like Meredith, but I didn't want Greg to hurt her. So I ran up and pushed him. He fell into the pool, and he hit his head." Aidy started to cry. "I tried to pull him out of the pool, but I couldn't."

"Why didn't you tell the police?" I asked.

"Because I kissed Greg earlier this year, then he went back to Meredith. And I'm not rich. The police don't listen to working class girls."

"You left the necklace for someone to find it," said Holiday, turning to Meredith. "And you scratched your own neck. You wanted the police to believe that you and Aidy fought. Then, you gave Aidy an alibi, and she gave you one back."

Reyes and O'Neal came to August House twenty minutes later. They asked us all a lot of questions, and then put Meredith and Aidy into the police car, and drove away.

"Are you ready to go?" said Holiday.

"Can you give me two minutes?" I said. "There's something I need to do."

Eliza was reading in the library.

"Hey," I said.

She looked up, then back at her book.

"I'm sorry, Eliza," I said. "I wasn't a good friend to you. I didn't see you as a real person, I only saw who I wanted to see. You deserve better than me. I hope we can be friends again one day."

"I don't," said Eliza, and laughed. "Goodbye."

I walked out of the library and into the garden to see Jasper. His eyes were wet. Was he crying?

"Hey," I said. "Are you OK?"

"I don't know," said Jasper quietly. "Greg and I were friends once. Did you know that?"

"I'm sorry, Jasper," I said. "I have something to tell you. I'm not rich. I have a scholarship, and I worked at a supermarket this summer."

Jasper looked at me. "I know," he said. "You try to be like us, but it shows. Life isn't a movie, Linden. I wasn't your friend because I thought that you were rich. Nobody cares about money but you."

I didn't think that was true, but I didn't say anything.

"I'm leaving now," I said.

"OK," said Jasper. "I'll see you at school."

"Yeah," I said, but I didn't yet know about my scholarship, and I didn't really believe that Jasper wanted to be my friend any more.

I waved at him, and then I walked away.

Holiday was waiting for me outside.

"I'm sorry, Holiday," I said as she drove me to the boat. "I was an asshole to you. And I don't just mean about last night. I'm sorry that I disappeared from your life."

"Yes, you were an asshole," said Holiday, but then she smiled. "But you can start being a friend now."

"I will," I said.

"Good," said Holiday. "See you later, Michael."

I climbed out of Holiday's car and walked to the boat. Before I got on it, I waved to her. Then, I looked at my phone in surprise. I had a message from Greer. It said: *Please call me. We need to talk.*

During-reading questions

CHAPTER ONE

1. Why does Linden lie to Jasper about his job?
2. How did Linden get into his expensive boarding school?
3. When did Linden hurt his leg and how did he do it?

CHAPTER TWO

1. Why does Linden take Holiday away from the rest of the group?
2. Does Linden want to get coffee with Holiday? Why/Why not?
3. Why does Jasper hate Meredith?

CHAPTER THREE

1. Why is Eliza in the library?
2. Who stops Wells's and Greg's fight? What happens to Greg next?

CHAPTER FOUR

1. Why does Linden feel different from the others on the island?
2. What books does Holiday read?
3. Why does Linden say, "No, thanks" when Holiday asks "Shall I take you back in my car?", do you think?

CHAPTER FIVE

1. Why does Holiday ask "Where's the bathroom?", do you think?
2. What clue do Linden and Holiday find in Wells's room?

CHAPTER SIX

1. Why does Eliza come to the street party?
2. What is Wells's secret?

CHAPTER SEVEN

1 Why does Linden decide to stay on the island?
2 How does Linden get to Holiday's house?
3 Where is Topher from and what does Greg do for him?

CHAPTER EIGHT

1 Why doesn't Linden want Holiday to come to the hurricane party now?
2 What does Linden find on Eliza's phone? Why does this change things for him?
3 Who is Linden jealous of?

CHAPTER NINE

1 Why does Linden go back to August House?
2 What did Meredith steal?
3 What happens to Meredith and Aidy?

After-reading questions

1 Linden lies a lot in this story, but is he a bad person because of this, do you think? Why/Why not?
2 Eliza says, "I couldn't tell you that I was at Doc's, because you were jealous of him." What other people is Linden jealous of in the story, do you think? Why is this?
3 Is Linden a good friend to Jasper, do you think? Why/Why not?
4 Look back at your answer to "Before-reading question 4". Were your answers right? Why/Why not?

Exercises

CHAPTER ONE

1 Complete these sentences in your notebook with the correct form of the verb.

1 Jasper ....*met*.... (meet) Linden at the boat.
2 Linden didn't want Jasper to .... (know) that his money impressed him.
3 Linden .... (see) Jasper's dog, Whimsy, sleeping in the hall.
4 Mr. Kendrick asked, "Are you going to .... (play) lacrosse in the fall?"
5 Jasper wanted to know why Meredith was .... (be) so rude.
6 Only two people .... (call) Linden by his first name.

CHAPTER TWO

2 Match the two parts of the sentences in your notebook.
Example: 1—c

1 She still had her dark curly hair and glasses,
2 I didn't want Eliza or Jasper to know
3 But I couldn't be angry at Jasper,
4 My parents are leaving the island to see some friends tonight,
5 I wanted to date her, but I told Greg,
6 I don't think that she'll be happy

a because I had big secrets too.
b and then he kissed her.
c but she looked older and prettier.
d to see Aidy at the party.
e that my mother worked for Holiday's parents.
f so we're having a party at August House.

CHAPTER THREE

3 **Complete the text in your notebook, using the words from the box.**

| knocked | coma | truth | lied | broken |

After they finished cleaning, Linden went upstairs and
¹ *knocked* on Eliza's bedroom door.
He and Eliza went downstairs the next morning and found Greg's body in the pool, so they called the police.
The police arrived and asked, "What other people were here last night?" but Eliza did not tell the ²............
Linden did not understand why she ³............ to the police.
Eliza asked, "Is Greg OK?" and the police officer said, "Greg is in a ⁴............"
Later, Linden found a ⁵............ necklace in the pool. It looked expensive. "Whose necklace is this?" Linden thought.

CHAPTER FOUR

4 **Are these sentences *true* or *false*? Correct the false sentences in your notebook.**

1 Linden thinks that somebody tried to kill Greg.
False. Linden thinks that it was an accident.

2 Linden is happy to see Holiday on the beach.

3 Linden tells the truth to Holiday about his leg.

4 Holiday thinks that someone moved Greg's body.

5 Doc stayed in Eliza's room until 3 a.m.

6 Holiday has her own car.

CHAPTER FIVE

5 Write questions for these answers in your notebook.
1. *Who thinks that Holiday looks pretty?* Linden and Wells think that she looks pretty.
2. She saw her at the music store.
3. No, Meredith doesn't think Aidy pushed Greg.
4. Her nails are white and short.
5. No, Linden doesn't remember Greg's clothes at the party.

CHAPTER SIX

6 Complete these sentences in your notebook, using the prepositions from the box.

with	behind	for	on

1. Linden went to the street party *with* the Kendricks.
2. When they got into town, Linden started to look .... Holiday, but he couldn't find her.
3. Eliza was sitting alone .... a wall.
4. Linden stood .... a tree.

CHAPTER SEVEN

7 Put the events of the story in the correct order in your notebook.
a. Holiday and Linden follow Topher to a cheap hotel. (........)
b. Linden tells Holiday that they need to keep investigating because Greg sells weed for someone in Boston. (........)
c. Linden and Holiday realise that Topher is innocent. (........)
d. Eliza asks Linden to stay on the island for the hurricane party. (...*1*...)

CHAPTER EIGHT

8 Write the correct question word. Then answer the questions in your notebook.

> who   what   how   where

1 ...*Who*... was Eliza playing a game with when Linden arrived?
   Eliza was playing a game with Doc when Linden arrived.
2 .... did Linden feel at the start of the party?
3 .... did Linden find Eliza?
4 .... did Eliza say to Linden about Greg?

CHAPTER NINE

9 Who is thinking this, do you think? Write the correct name in your notebook.

1 "All my friends hate me because I investigated them." ...*Linden*...
2 "I need to get out of here before the police come."
3 "Why is Linden back here?"
4 "I don't want to talk to Linden ever again."

Project work

1 Write a newspaper article about the murder at August House.
2 Holiday loves mystery books. Think of a mystery book that Holiday might enjoy. Write three reasons why she might enjoy it.
3 Write a review of this book. Did you like it? Why/Why not?

An answer key for all questions and exercises can be found at **www.penguinreaders.co.uk**

Glossary

accident (n.)
A bad thing happens and then someone is hurt. No one planned this thing. It was an *accident*.

accuse (v.)
to say that a person has done something wrong

alibi (n.)
You were in another place or with a person when something bad happened. You didn't do it. You have an *alibi*.

alone (adj.)
You have no one with you. You are *alone*.

asshole (n.)
a bad or *rude* word for a stupid person

believe (v.)
to be sure that something is real or true

blood (n.)
Blood goes around your body and comes out if you cut your body. *Blood* is red.

boarding school (n.)
an expensive school. Parents pay for their children to live at a *boarding school*.

bribe (v. and n.)
You give money to someone and they do something (it is usually bad) to help you. You *bribe* the person. This is a *bribe*.

broken (adj.)
A *broken* thing is in small bits after an *accident*.

cheat on (phr. v.)
If you *cheat on* your boyfriend, girlfriend, husband or wife, you have sex with a different person.

coma (n.)
A person is in a *coma* when they are very ill in hospital. They are sleeping and do not wake up. Doctors sometimes try to wake them up.

crash (n.)
One thing hits another thing, for example, a car has a *crash* with another car.

date (v.)
If you *date* someone, they are your boyfriend or girlfriend.

deserve (v.)
If someone *deserves* something, it is right that they get it because they did good or bad things.

disappear (v.)
a person is there and you can see them. Then you cannot see them. They *disappeared*.

embarrassed (adj.);
embarrassing (adj.)
If you are *embarrassed*, you are feeling worried because you did something bad or stupid. If something is *embarrassing*, you feel *embarrassed* about it.

grin (n. and v.)
A *grin* is a big smile. To *grin* is to smile in this way.

hurricane (n.)
a big storm made from warm air. *Hurricanes* have very strong wind and heavy rain.

impress (v.)
If something *impresses* you, you like it because it is interesting, clever or beautiful.

innocent (adj.)
If you are *innocent*, you did not do something bad.

investigate (v.)
to try to get information about someone, or about something bad that has happened

jealous (adj.)
You love someone but they love another person, and then you are not happy. You are *jealous* of that person.

knock (v.)
You hit a door with the back of your fingers and make a noise. People behind the door know you are there because you *knocked* on the door.

law (n.)
The *law* is the right and wrong things to do in a country. If you have studied *law*, you might get a *law* job. If you have trouble with the *law*, the police are *investigating* you. They think that you have done something wrong.

lie (n. and v.); **liar** (n.)
You say something but it is not true. You are *lying* or telling a *lie*. If you do this, you are a *liar*.

mystery (n.)
If you cannot explain something, it is a *mystery*.

nail (n.)
the hard, flat part at the end of your finger

obsessed (adj.); **obsession** (n.)
if you are *obsessed* with someone or something, you think about them all the time. This is an *obsession*.

owe (v.)
You borrow money from someone. Then you *owe* the person money. You must give it back.

pretend (v.)
to act like something is true when it is not

prove (v.)
to show that something is true

regret (v.)
to feel sad or sorry about something that you did or did not do

research (v.)
You *research* something when you try to find information about it.

rude (adj.)
not speaking or acting in a nice way

scholarship (n.)
If you are given a *scholarship*, you can study at an expensive school without paying.

scratch (v. and n.)
If you *scratch* someone, you hurt their body with your *nails*. Then there is a red line on their body. This is a *scratch*.

security (n.)
Security things and people keep you safe. A *security* camera is a video camera. It makes a film. If a bad thing happens, the police can watch the video to see who did it.

solve (v.)
to find a good answer to a problem

suspect (n.)
The police *investigate* someone because maybe they did something wrong. This person is a *suspect*.

truth (n.)
The *truth* is what really happened. *Truth* is the noun of true.

view (n.)
You can see something beautiful, for example the sea or some mountains. You have a beautiful *view*.

weed (n.)
a word for cannabis (Cannabis is made from the leaves of a plant. People smoke it or eat it.

working class (adj.)
Working class people often have less money than others. They often work in manual (= using their hands, etc.) jobs.